# Activity Book for Children
## Christopher Clark
## Illustrated by Alex Brychta

**6**

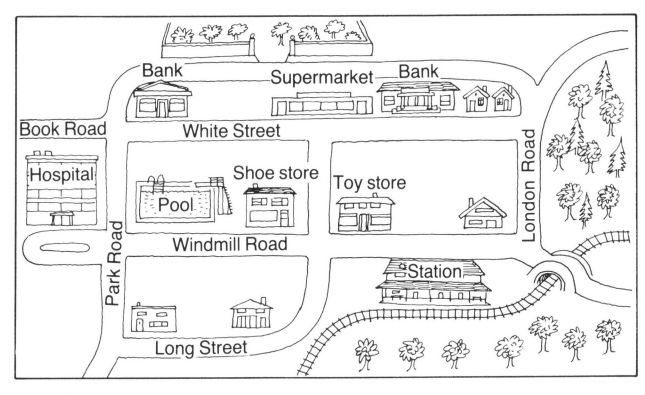

## Draw in these buildings

There is a school on Park Road. It is between the park and Book Road.

There is a big supermarket on Windmill Road. It is opposite the pool and the shoe store.

There is a hotel on Park Road. It is next to the hospital.

There is a bus stop on Windmill Road. It is opposite the station.

There is a book store on White Street. It is next to the little bank.

**Yes, there is.　　No, there isn't.**

Is there a toy store near your school?　　_ _ _ _ _ _ _ _ _ _

Is there a station near your school?　　_ _ _ _ _ _ _ _ _ _

Is there a police station near your school?　_ _ _ _ _ _ _ _ _ _

Is there a park near your house?　　_ _ _ _ _ _ _ _ _ _

Is there a river near your house?　　_ _ _ _ _ _ _ _ _ _

Is there a river near your teacher's house?　_ _ _ _ _ _ _ _ _ _

Is there a bank near your teacher's house?　_ _ _ _ _ _ _ _ _ _

Is there an ice cream store near your school?_ _ _ _ _ _ _ _ _

# CAN YOU READ?

frog
tree

dress
present

brush
trumpet

crash
drinking

tree
drinking

trumpet
frog

crash
present

brush
dress

# WHAT IS DIFFERENT?

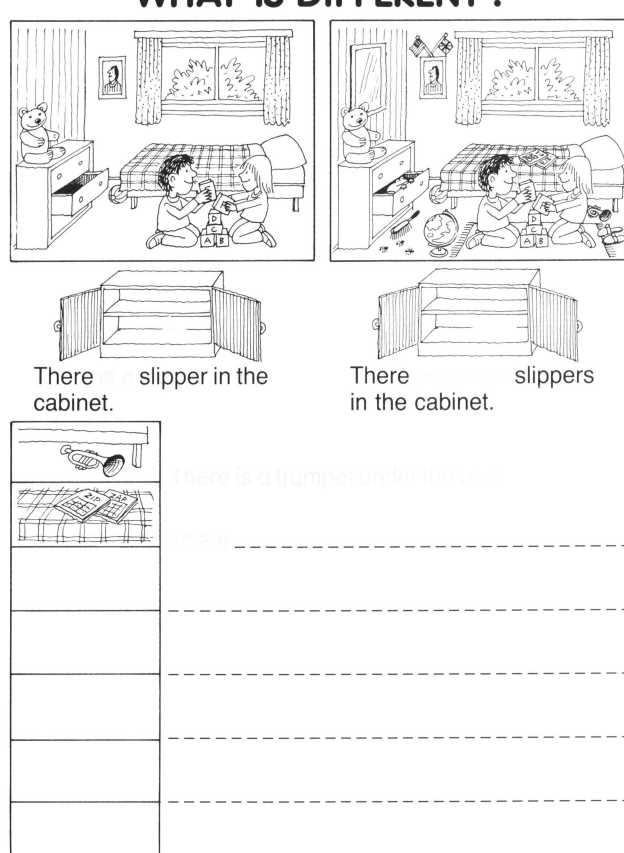

There is a slipper in the cabinet.

There are two slippers in the cabinet.

There is a trumpet under the bed.

There _____

_____

_____

_____

_____

_____

ants    brush    rug    comics    drawer    flags    floor    frog
globe    in front of    mirror    near    on    picture    wall

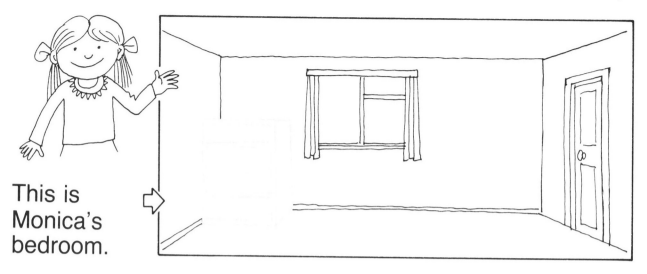

This is Monica's bedroom.

There is a tall white bookcase in the corner. There are a lot of books and comics. There is a green desk under the window. It is very messy. There is an old chair in front of the desk.

There is a brown bed between the door and the desk. The blankets are yellow and red. There are two dolls on the bed. There is a picture of a dog on the wall. There is a green rug on the floor.

Draw your room.

There is a _ _ _ _ _ _ _ _ _ _ _ _ _ _ _ _ _ _ _ _ _ _ _ _ _ _ _ _ _ _ _ _ _ _ _ _ _ _ _

_ _ _ _ _ _ _ _ _ _ _ _ _ _ _ _ _ _ _ _ _ _ _ _ _ _ _ _ _ _ _ _ _ _ _ _ _ _ _ _ _ _ _ _ _ _ _

_ _ _ _ _ _ _ _ _ _ _ _ _ _ _ _ _ _ _ _ _ _ _ _ _ _ _ _ _ _ _ _ _ _ _ _ _ _ _ _ _ _ _ _ _ _ _

_ _ _ _ _ _ _ _ _ _ _ _ _ _ _ _ _ _ _ _ _ _ _ _ _ _ _ _ _ _ _ _ _ _ _ _ _ _ _ _ _ _ _ _ _ _ _

_ _ _ _ _ _ _ _ _ _ _ _ _ _ _ _ _ _ _ _ _ _ _ _ _ _ _ _ _ _ _ _ _ _ _ _ _ _ _ _ _ _ _ _ _ _ _

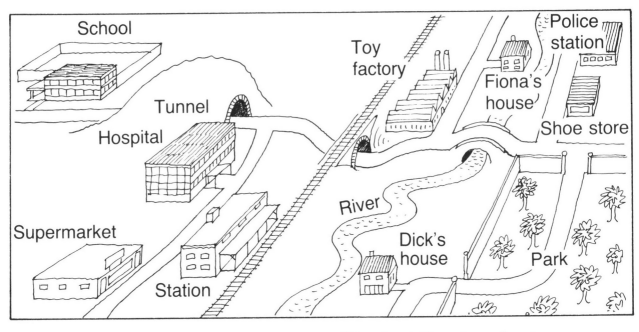

Start at the school.
Go through the tunnel.
Turn right.
Go past the hospital.
Where are you?

station

Start at the police station.
Go past the shoe store.
Turn left.
Go through the park.
Where are you?

- - - - - - - - - - - - - - - - - - -

Start at the toy factory.
Turn left.
Cross the river.
Turn left.
Where are you?

- - - - - - - - - - - - - - - - - - -

Start at the station.
Go past the hospital.
Turn right.
Go under the bridge.
Turn left.
Where are you?

- - - - - - - - - - - - - - - - - - -

Now you write.

- - - - - - - - - - - - - - - - - - -

- - - - - - - - - - - - - - - - - - -

- - - - - - - - - - - - - - - - - - -

- - - - - - - - - - - - - - - - - - -

- - - - - - - - - - - - - - - - - - -

c a k e          r o s e          k i t e

b i k e          p i n          g a t e          p a n

d o g          n o s e          f i v e          m a p

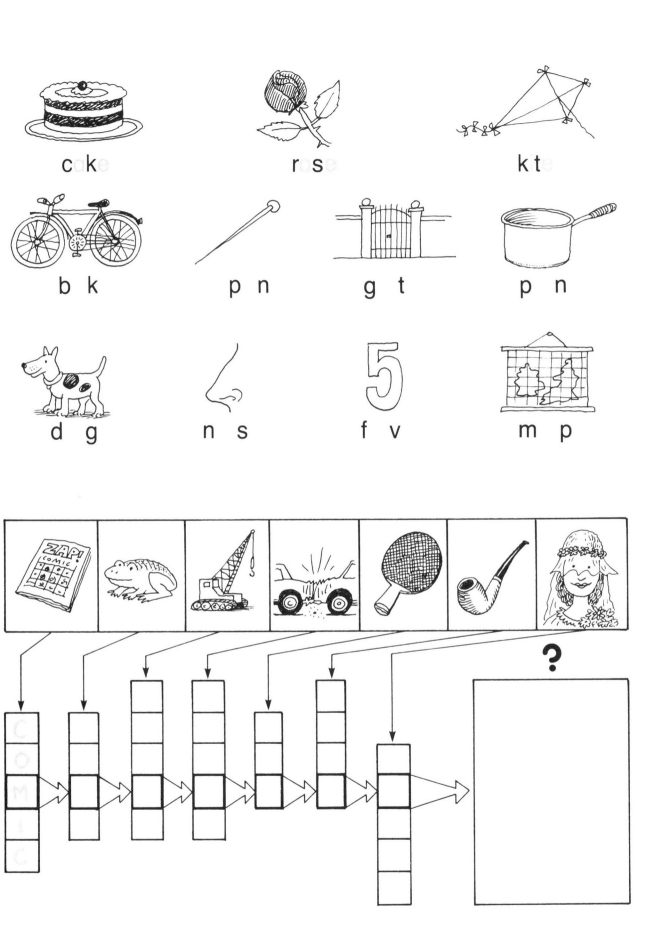

?

7

Make your own park. Choose four attractions

Is there a clown in your park?

Are there any teachers?

Are there any go-carts?      _____

Is there a roller coaster?      _____

Is there a hall of mirrors?      _____

Are there any animals?      _____

Is there a Ferris wheel?      _____

Which attraction do you like best?

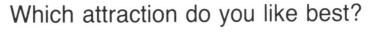

Which attraction does your teacher like best?

_____

Is there a slide?
Yes, there is.

Are there any clowns?
No, there aren't.

Are there any swings?
Yes, there are.

Is _ _ _ _ _ _ _ hall of mirrors?
No, there isn't.

Is _ _ _ _ _ _ _ _ _ _ _ _ _ _ _ _ _ _ _

_ _ _ _ _ _ _ _ _ _ Yes, there is.

_ _ _ _ _ _ _ _ _ _ _ _ _ _ _ _ _ _ _ _

_ _ _ _ _ _ _ _ No, there aren't.

_ _ _ _ _ _ _ _ _ _ _ _ _ _ _ _ _ _

_ _ _ _ _ _ No, there isn't.

_ _ _ _ _ _ _ _ _ _ _ _ _ _ _ _ _ _ _ _

_ _ _ _ _ _ _ _ Yes, there are.

# START

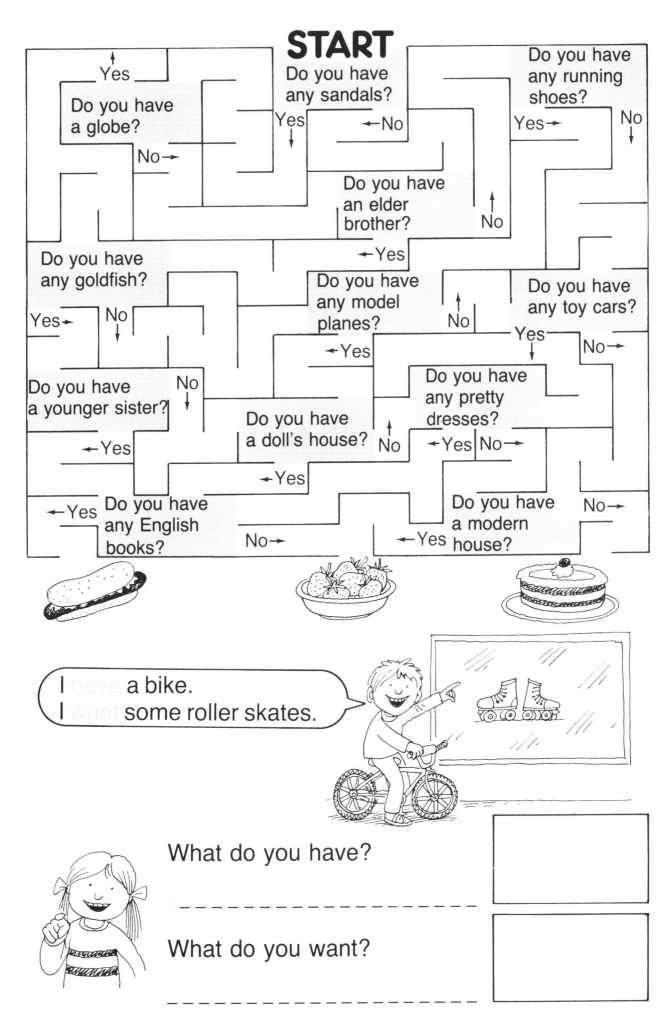

Do you have any sandals?

Do you have a globe?

Do you have any running shoes?

Do you have an elder brother?

Do you have any goldfish?

Do you have any model planes?

Do you have any toy cars?

Do you have a younger sister?

Do you have any pretty dresses?

Do you have a doll's house?

Do you have any English books?

Do you have a modern house?

I have a bike.
I want some roller skates.

What do you have?

What do you want?

10

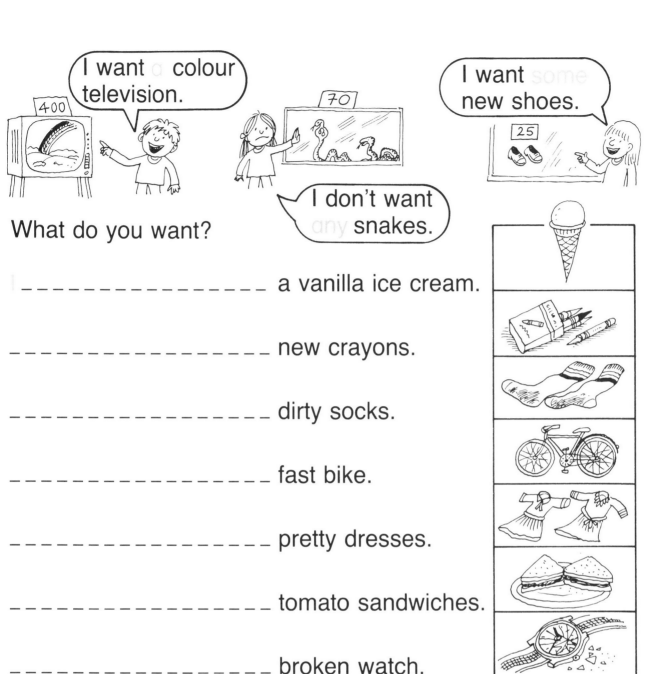

I want a colour television.

I want some new shoes.

I don't want any snakes.

What do you want?

I _ _ _ _ _ _ _ _ _ _ _ _ _ _ a vanilla ice cream.

_ _ _ _ _ _ _ _ _ _ _ _ _ _ new crayons.

_ _ _ _ _ _ _ _ _ _ _ _ _ _ dirty socks.

_ _ _ _ _ _ _ _ _ _ _ _ _ _ fast bike.

_ _ _ _ _ _ _ _ _ _ _ _ _ _ pretty dresses.

_ _ _ _ _ _ _ _ _ _ _ _ _ _ tomato sandwiches.

_ _ _ _ _ _ _ _ _ _ _ _ _ _ broken watch.

# CAN YOU FIND THESE THINGS?

| S | T | K | R | P | C | A | N | E |
| M | A | P | E | O | I | R | T | R | O | S |
| N | P | I | P | E | S | N | A | K | E | B | N | V |
| R | A | B | B | I | T | E | E | N | R | C | R | A | S | H |
| O | P | I | P | N | C | A | M | E | L | S | A | K | E | P |

 Jane and Peter leave home at 7:55.

Steve leaves home at 8:00.

Jane and Peter meet Carol at the bus stop.

They catch the 8:15 bus.

They arrive at school at 8:30.

Steve walks through the park.

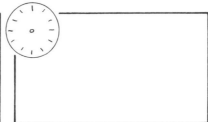

He arrives at 8:30.

School starts at 8:45.

How long does Steve take to go to school?

He takes thirty minutes.

How long do Jane and Peter take?

They _ _ _ _ _ _ _ _ _ _ _ _ _ _ _ _ _ _ _ _ _ _ _ _ _ _ _ _ _ _

How long do you take?

_ _ _ _ _ _ _ _ _ _ _ _ _ _ _ _ _ _ _ _ _ _ _ _ _ _ _ _ _ _ _

How long does your teacher take?

_ _ _ _ _ _ _ _ _ _ _ _ _ _ _ _ _ _ _ _ _ _ _ _ _ _ _ _ _ _ _

| one | two | three | four | five | six | seven | eight | nine | ten |
|---|---|---|---|---|---|---|---|---|---|
| eleven | twelve | thirteen | fourteen | fifteen | sixteen | seventeen | eighteen | | |

nineteen

| twenty | thirty | forty | fifty | sixty | seventy | eighty | ninety |
|---|---|---|---|---|---|---|---|

Draw today's
weather. ⇨

| sunny  windy  raining  snowing  cloudy |

|  |  |  |  |
|---|---|---|---|
|  |  |  |  |

How do you go to school?

I leave _ _ _ _ _ _ _ _ _ _ _ _ _ _ _ _ _ _ _ _ _ _ _ _ _

_ _ _ _ _ _ _ _ _ _ _ _ _ _ _ _ _ _ _ _ _ _ _ _ _ _ _ _

_ _ _ _ _ _ _ _ _ _ _ _ _ _ _ _ _ _ _ _ _ _ _ _ _ _ _ _

_ _ _ _ _ _ _ _ _ _ _ _ _ _ _ _ _ _ _ _ _ _ _ _ _ _ _ _

# CAN YOU READ?

| sleep | | flag | | glass | |
|---|---|---|---|---|---|
| slide | | flower | | globe | |
| slippers | | flame | | glasses | |

| blanket | | plus | | clock | |
|---|---|---|---|---|---|
| blackboard | | plane | | clown | |
| black | | playing | | classroom | |

| Monday | Tuesday | Wednesday | Thursday |
|--------|---------|-----------|----------|
| Friday | Saturday | Sunday | |

She eats rice everyday.
She sometimes drinks apple juice.
She never eats carrots.

She sometimes eats _ _ _ _ _ _ _ _ _ _ _ _ _ _ _ _ _ _

She _ _ _ _ _ _ _ _ _ _ _ _ _ _ _ _ _ _ _ _ _ _ _ _ _ _ _

_ _ _ _ _ _ _ _ _ _ _ _ _ _ _ _ _ _ _ _ _ _ _ _ _ _ _

_ _ _ _ _ _ _ _ _ _ _ _ _ _ _ _ _ _ _ _ _ _ _ _ _ _ _

_ _ _ _ _ _ _ _ _ _ _ _ _ _ _ _ _ _ _ _ _ _ _ _ _ _ _

What do you eat and drink?

I _ _ _ _ _ _ _ _ _ _ _ _ _ _ eat _ _ _ _ _ _ _ _ _ _ _ _ _

_ _ _ _ _ _ _ _ _ _ _ _ _ _ _ _ _ _ _ _ _ _ _ _ _ _ _

bread  cake  chicken  fish  hamburgers  ice cream  milk  water

14

**never**     **sometimes**     **everyday**

How often do you wash your face?     everyday

How often do you play in the park?     _ _ _ _ _ _ _ _ _ _ _ _ _ _

How often do you ride a bike?     _ _ _ _ _ _ _ _ _ _ _ _ _ _

How often do you watch television?     _ _ _ _ _ _ _ _ _ _ _ _ _ _

How often do you drink milk?     _ _ _ _ _ _ _ _ _ _ _ _ _ _

How often do you listen to the radio?     _ _ _ _ _ _ _ _ _ _ _ _ _ _

How often do you wash your hands?     _ _ _ _ _ _ _ _ _ _ _ _ _ _

How often do you read comics?     _ _ _ _ _ _ _ _ _ _ _ _ _ _

How often do you sleep in class?     _ _ _ _ _ _ _ _ _ _ _ _ _ _

# CROSSWORD PUZZLE

### Across ➡
**1** The day between Wednesday and Friday.
**5** The last day of the week.
**6** The fourth day of the week.

### Down ⬇
**1** The day before Wednesday.
**2** The first day of the week.
**3** The day after Thursday.
**4** The second day of the week.

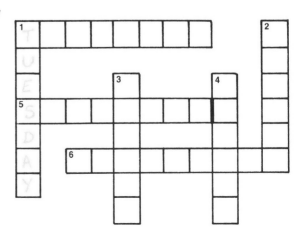

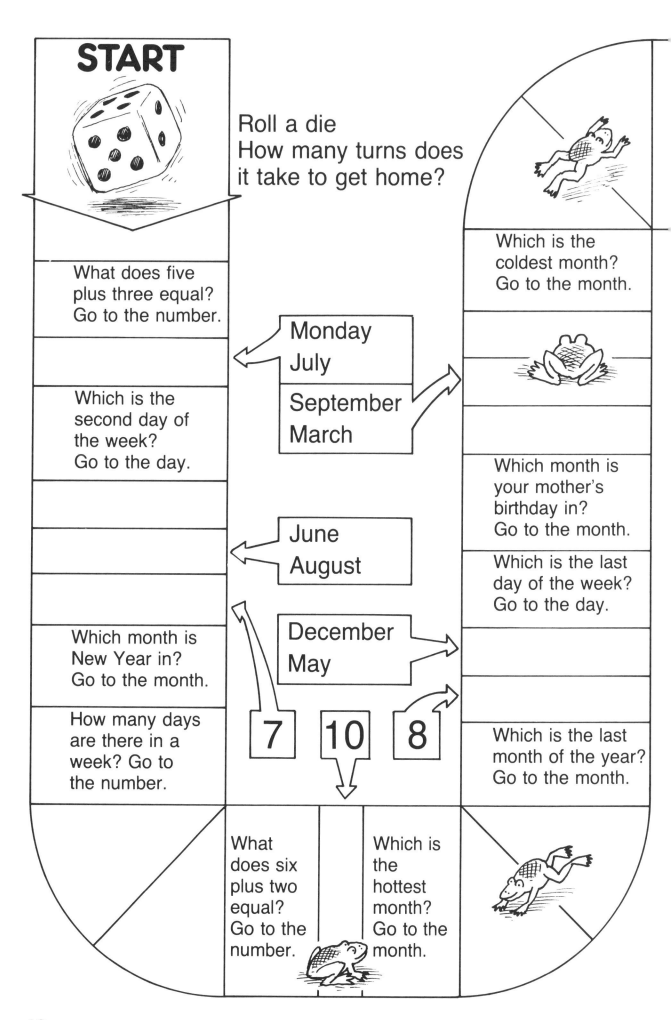

**START**

Roll a die
How many turns does it take to get home?

What does five plus three equal? Go to the number.

Which is the second day of the week? Go to the day.

Which month is New Year in? Go to the month.

How many days are there in a week? Go to the number.

Monday
July
September
March

June
August

December
May

7  10  8

Which is the coldest month? Go to the month.

Which month is your mother's birthday in? Go to the month.

Which is the last day of the week? Go to the day.

Which is the last month of the year? Go to the month.

What does six plus two equal? Go to the number.

Which is the hottest month? Go to the month.

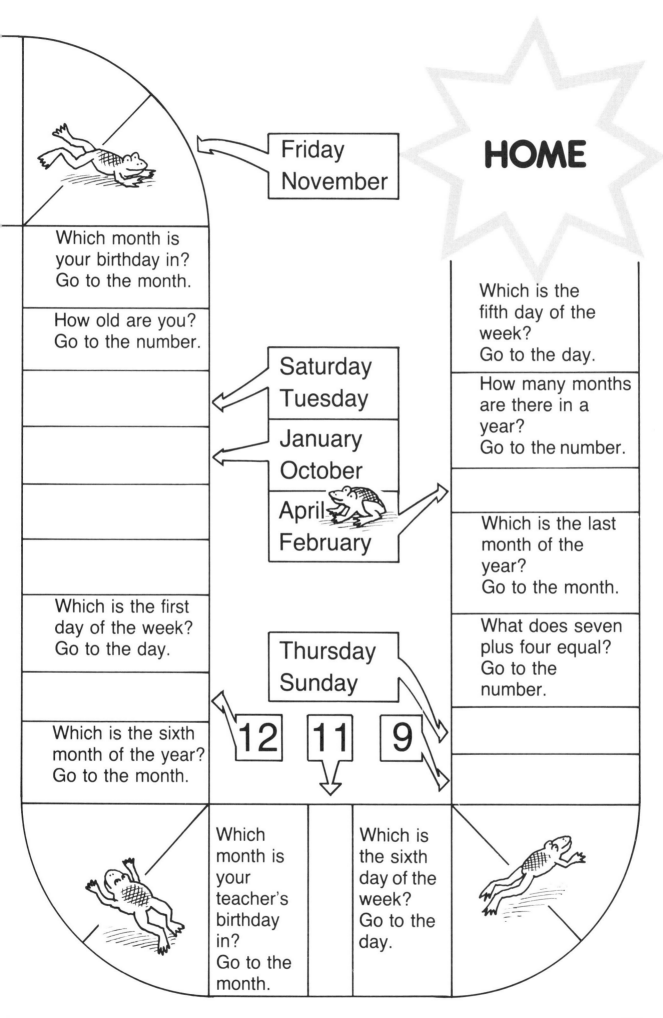

Friday
November

**HOME**

Which month is your birthday in? Go to the month.

How old are you? Go to the number.

Which is the fifth day of the week? Go to the day.

How many months are there in a year? Go to the number.

Saturday
Tuesday

January
October

April
February

Which is the last month of the year? Go to the month.

What does seven plus four equal? Go to the number.

Which is the first day of the week? Go to the day.

Thursday
Sunday

Which is the sixth month of the year? Go to the month.

12  11  9

Which month is your teacher's birthday in? Go to the month.

Which is the sixth day of the week? Go to the day.

Vanessa's mother can ride a horse and drive a car but she can't cook.

Her grandmother can't skate or ride a bike but she can play the trumpet.

Her younger sister can cook and she can play the piano and skip.

Her father can drive a car but he can't ride a bike or skate.

Her elder sister can play the piano and drive a car but she can't ride a bike.

Her brother can't cook but he can play the piano and the trumpet.

What can you do?

I can _____

_____

What can't you do?

_____

_____

18

Today's date: _ _ _ _ _ _ _ _ _ _ _ _ _ _ _ _ _ _ _ _ _

Draw today's weather. ⇨

| sunny   windy   raining   snowing   cloudy |

Write about your family.

My _ _ _ _ _ can _ _ _ _ _ _ _ _ _ _ _ _ _ _ _ _ _ _ _

but _ _ _ _ _ can't _ _ _ _ _ _ _ _ _ _ _ _ _ _ _ _ _ _

_ _ _ _ _ _ _ _ _ _ _ _ _ _ _ _ _ _ _ _ _ _ _ _ _ _ _ _ _ _

_ _ _ _ _ _ _ _ _ _ _ _ _ _ _ _ _ _ _ _ _ _ _ _ _ _ _ _ _ _

_ _ _ _ _ _ _ _ _ _ _ _ _ _ _ _ _ _ _ _ _ _ _ _ _ _ _ _ _ _

# CAN YOU READ?

smoke

star

sleep

swim

snake

skates

skates    slide

swim      stop

smoke     spoon

sleep     snow

star      slipper

snake     street

snow

spoon

stop

slide

street

slipper

19

| 462 | 571 | 398 |
|---|---|---|
| four hundred and sixty-two | five hundred and seventy-one | three hundred and ninety-eight |

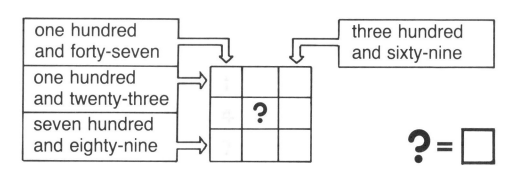

one hundred and forty-seven

three hundred and sixty-nine

one hundred and twenty-three

seven hundred and eighty-nine

? = ☐

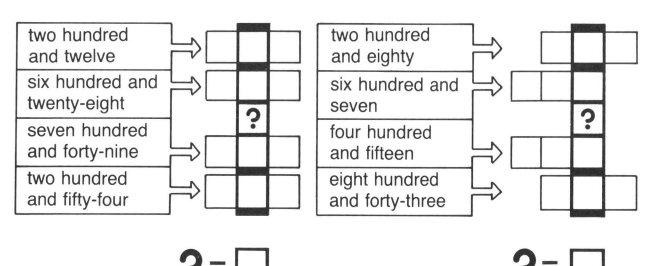

two hundred and twelve

six hundred and twenty-eight

seven hundred and forty-nine

two hundred and fifty-four

? = ☐

two hundred and eighty

six hundred and seven

four hundred and fifteen

eight hundred and forty-three

? = ☐

What number is after 781?     seven hundred and _ _ _ _ _ _ _ _ _ _ _ _ _ _

What does 582 plus 47 equal?     _ _ _ _ _ _ _ _ _ _ _ _ _ _ _ _ _ _ _ _ _ _ _

What number is between
507 and 509?     _ _ _ _ _ _ _ _ _ _ _ _ _ _ _ _ _ _ _ _ _ _ _

Which is bigger 471 or 338?     _ _ _ _ _ _ _ _ _ _ _ _ _ _ _ _ _ _ _ _ _ _

What number is before 352?     _ _ _ _ _ _ _ _ _ _ _ _ _ _ _ _ _ _ _ _ _ _

Which is smaller 765 or 665?     _ _ _ _ _ _ _ _ _ _ _ _ _ _ _ _ _ _ _ _ _ _

Today's date: _____

Draw today's weather. ⇨

sunny   windy   raining   snowing   cloudy

# PICTURE PUZZLE

crab

_ _ _ _ _ _     _ _ _ _ _ _     _ _ _ _ _ _

_ _ _ _ _ _     _ _ _ _ _ _     _ _ _ _ _ _

_ _ _ _ _ _     _ _ _ _ _ _     _ _ _ _ _ _     _ _ _ _ _ _

Nick cleans his room twice a day. His room is very neat.

Barbara washes her father's car three times a week. The car is very clean.

In winter Rose watches television for five hours every day. Her eyes are square.

In summer Helen and David go to the beach every Saturday. They are very happy.

Henry brushes his teeth only once a month. His teeth are very bad.

Alice never cleans her shoes. Her shoes are the dirtiest in the school.

once        a day
twice       a week
three times a month
four times  a year

How often do you have a birthday?        once a year

How often do you brush your hair?        _ _ _ _ _ _ _ _ _ _ _

How often do you clean your room?        _ _ _ _ _ _ _ _ _ _ _

How often do you have English lessons?   _ _ _ _ _ _ _ _ _ _ _

How often do you have a test in school?  _ _ _ _ _ _ _ _ _ _ _

How often do you clean your shoes?       _ _ _ _ _ _ _ _ _ _ _

How often do you have homework?          _ _ _ _ _ _ _ _ _ _ _

How often do you brush your teeth?

_ _ _ _ _ _ _ _ _ _ _ _ _ _ _ _ _ _ _ _ _ _

Make sets.

HOUSE  SCHOOL  STORE  POLICE STATION  WOMAN  ZOO  KANGAROO
MONKEY  POLICEMAN  BABY  MIRROR  ALLIGATOR  BOOKCASE  CHAIR  SNAKE
TEACHER  OCTOPUS  RUG  TABLE  GRANDFATHER

_ _ _ _ _ _ _   _ _ _ _ _ _ _   _ _ _ _ _ _ _

_ _ _ _ _ _ _   _ _ _ _ _ _ _   _ _ _ _ _ _ _

table    _ _ _ _ _ _ _   _ _ _ _ _ _ _   _ _ _ _ _ _ _

_ _ _ _ _ _ _   _ _ _ _ _ _ _   _ _ _ _ _ _ _

_ _ _ _ _ _ _   _ _ _ _ _ _ _   _ _ _ _ _ _ _   _ _ _ _ _ _ _

# TV GUIDE

| Tuesday | Wednesday | Thursday |
|---|---|---|
| 4:40 Pet Corner | 4:35 English | 4:40 Star Watch |
| 5:10 _ _ _ _ _ _ _ | 4:50 _ _ _ _ _ _ _ | 5:00 _ _ _ _ _ _ _ |
| 5:35 _ _ _ _ _ _ _ | 5:40 Super Car | 5:15 _ _ _ _ _ _ _ |
| 6:00 _ _ _ _ _ _ _ | 6:00 _ _ _ _ _ _ _ | 6:00 _ _ _ _ _ _ _ |

Animal Safari is on Wednesday before Super Car.
The Monster Game is on Thursday after Star Watch.
Big Cartoon is on Tuesday before the News.
Animal Quiz is on Thursday.
The News is at six o'clock every day.
Zappadak is on Tuesday after Pet Corner.

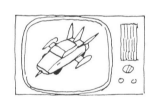 When is Super Car on?

It is on Wednesday at 5:40.

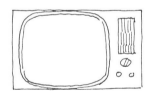 When is Big Cartoon on?

_ _ _ _ _ _ _ _ _ _ _ _ _ _ _ _ _ _ _ _ _ _ _ _ _ _ _ _ _ _

 When is the Monster Game on?

_ _ _ _ _ _ _ _ _ _ _ _ _ _ _ _ _ _ _ _ _ _ _ _ _ _ _ _ _ _

 What is your favorite program?

It is _ _ _ _ _ _ _ _ _ _ _ _ _ _ _ _ _ _ _ _ _ _ _ _ _ _ _

When is it on?

_ _ _ _ _ _ _ _ _ _ _ _ _ _ _ _ _ _ _ _ _ _ _ _ _ _ _ _ _ _

Sunday   Monday   Tuesday   Wednesday   Thursday   Friday   Saturday

Terry's favorite program is Martian Mike.
Martian Mike is from outer space.

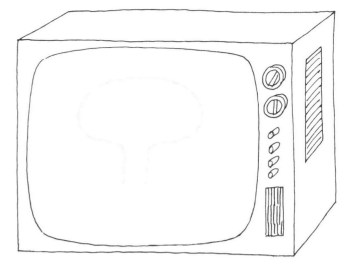

He has a big round head and a long straight neck. He has two big eyes and a funny little mouth. He doesn't have a nose or any ears, but he has a short antenna on the top of his head.

He has a little body and three short curly legs. He has a long thin arm.
His body is light green and his head, arm, neck and legs are yellow. He eats ants and bees. He doesn't drink anything.

Draw your own Martian.

My Martian has _____

_____

_____

_____

_____

# WHAT IS DIFFERENT?

There is a lamp on _ _ _ _ _ _ _ _ _ _ _ _ _ _ _ _ _ _

The man is wearing _ _ _ _ _ _ _ _ _ _ _ _ _ _ _ _ _

The woman's slippers _ _ _ _ _ _ _ _ _ _ _ _ _ _ _ _

_ _ _ _ _ _ _ _ _ _ _ _ _ _ _ _ _ _ _ _ _ _ _ _ _ _ _

_ _ _ _ _ _ _ _ _ _ _ _ _ _ _ _ _ _ _ _ _ _ _ _ _ _ _

_ _ _ _ _ _ _ _ _ _ _

bell    black    cat    hair    piano    picture    short    tie    wall

26

# MEMORY GAME

Look at the picture on the left.
Then hold your book like this.

| | Yes, there is. | No, there isn't. |
|---|---|---|
| Is there a light? | Yes, there is. | No, there isn't. |
| Is the cat sleeping? | Yes, it is. | No, it isn't. |
| Is the woman's sweater too big? | Yes, it is. | No, it isn't. |
| Are there any roses on the piano? | Yes, there are. | No, there aren't. |
| Is the man looking at the cat? | Yes, he is. | No, he isn't. |
| Are the man's jeans too long? | Yes, they are. | No, they aren't. |
| Is there a mirror on the wall? | Yes, there is. | No, there isn't. |
| Is the cat's tail very long? | Yes, it is. | No, it isn't. |
| Is the woman wearing a watch? | Yes, she is. | No, she isn't. |
| Are the man's glasses too big? | Yes, they are. | No, they aren't. |
| Is there a rug? | Yes, there is. | No, there isn't. |

# CAN YOU FIND THESE THINGS?

| P | G | R | A | P | E | S | P | P |
| P | L | A | N | E | U | T | P | L | A | T |
| C | R | A | B | E | S | H | E | P | A | N | E | T |
| P | O | O | N | I | T | E | E | T | H | T | B | U | S | E |
| R | O | S | E | S | D | I | S | H | E | E | P | R | A | S |

If your hair is green go down. If not, go right.

If two plus five equals seven go left. If not, go down.

If there are thirty-two pages in this book go up. If not, go down.

If you have a sister go left. If not, go right.

If your teacher can read go right. If not, go left.

If you have a nose go up. If not, go down.

If you like ice cream go right. If not, go up.

If you can read go up. If not, go right.

If you are wearing purple go up. If not, go left.

If you get up before six o'clock go up. If not, go left.

If there is a door in the room go up. If not, go down.

If your shoes are brown go up. If not, go left.

If you are the tallest in the class go up. If not, go right.

If one plus four equals five go up. If not, go down.

If you are wearing a skirt go up. If not, go right.

If it is cloudy go up. If not, go right.

If you can see a book go up. If not, go left.

If you can skip go left. If not, go up.

If you have six legs go right. If not, go up.

If you are a girl go right. If not, go left.

If you have three hands go left. If not, go up.

up

left    right

down

START

28

Today's date: _ _ _ _ _ _ _ _ _ _ _ _ _ _ _ _ _ _

Draw today's weather. ⇨

| sunny   windy   raining   snowing   cloudy |

## Across ➡

**1** What is the opposite of thin?
**4** What does five plus four equal?
**6** Look at page 5. What color is Monica's bookcase?
**8** Look at page 6. What is between the bridge and the school?
**9** What is the opposite of dirty?
**10** What is the third month?
**11** Look at page 14. What does she never eat?

## Down ⬇

**2** Look at page 25. What is on Martian Mike's head?
**3** Look at the man on page 26. What is different?
**5** Look at page 24. What is on before Animal Safari?
**7** Look at page 2. What is next to the hospital?
**9** You can read it. It is very funny. What is it?

In this book:

How many pages are there?                    _ _ _ _ _ _ _ _

How many skates can you find?                _ _ _ _ _ _ _ _

How many trumpets can you find?              _ _ _ _ _ _ _ _

How many boys and girls can you find?        _ _ _ _ _ _ _ _

Which is the best page?                      _ _ _ _ _ _ _ _

Today's date:_____

Draw today's
weather.  ⇨

| sunny windy raining snowing cloudy |

There is a clown.

There are some clowns.

Two hundred and fifty-six

Two hundred and sixty-five

There aren't any zebras.

There is an elephant.

She never drinks milk.

She sometimes drinks milk.

He catches the bus.

He walks through the park.

They are eating bananas.

They want some bananas.

He wants the bike.

He isn't wearing a watch.

She can knit.

She is knitting.

She has a trumpet.

She can't play the trumpet.

Saturday  Thursday  Monday  Wednesday  Friday  Tuesday

**1** Sunday

**2** _____

**3** _____

**4** _____

**5** _____

**6** _____

**7** _____

| | |
|---|---|
| Do you have green hair? | Yes, I do. | No, I don't. |
| Are you a girl? | Yes, I am. | No, I'm not. |
| Can you run? | Yes, I can. | No, I can't. |
| Are you wearing a hat? | Yes, I am. | No, I'm not. |
| Is there a bookcase in your classroom? | Yes, there is. | No, there isn't. |
| Can you see a boy? | Yes, I can. | No, I can't. |
| Are you the tallest in your class? | Yes, I am. | No, I'm not. |
| Does a fish have legs? | Yes, it does. | No, it doesn't. |
| Are there any books in your classroom? | Yes, there are. | No, there aren't. |
| Do you eat a banana every day? | Yes, I do. | No, I don't. |
| Can a snake play the piano? | Yes, it can. | No, it can't. |
| Do you have an English lesson every day? | Yes, I do. | No, I don't. |

# WHICH ONE IS DIFFERENT?

| | | | |
|---|---|---|---|
| dress  sock <br> pipe <br> jacket  jeans | dish  spoon <br> plate <br> comic  glass | hot dog  salad <br> cake <br> chicken  button | star  rug <br> mirror <br> bed  bookcase |
| October  June <br> November <br> April  Thursday | snake alligator <br> octopus <br> trumpet  frog | bank  hospital <br> street <br> hotel  toy store | lemon  carrots <br> banana <br> apple  peach |

31

Start from home. Go to the Boys' School, to a bike store, to Alan's house, to the park, to Linda's house, to a bakery, to a bike store, to a bakery, to the Girls' School and back to home.

**You can go along each road only once.**

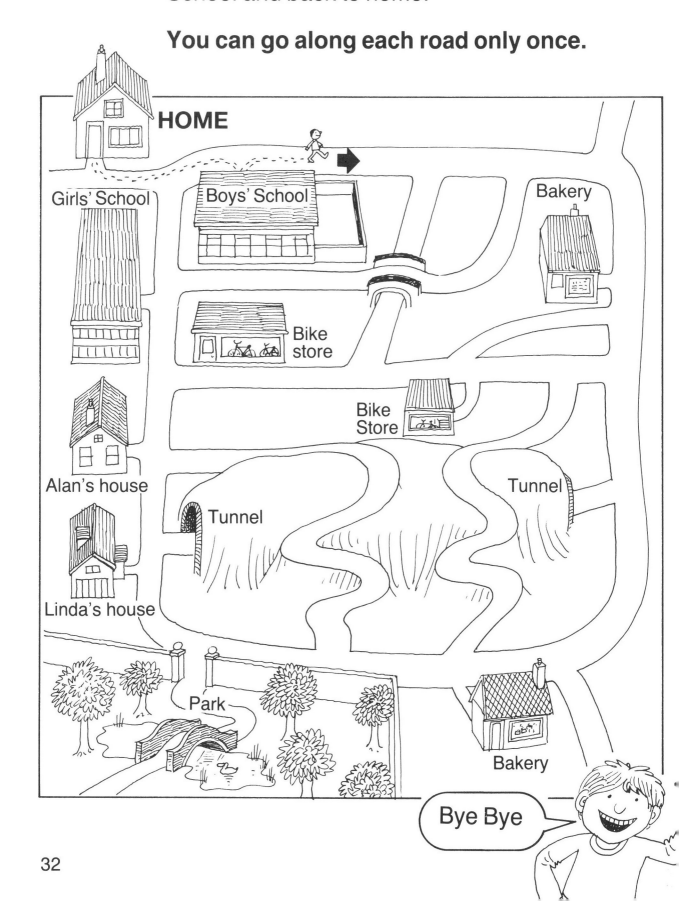